ABORIGINAL AUSTRALIANS

Diana Marshall

WEIGL PUBLISHERS INC.

Published by Weigl Publishers Inc.
350 5th Avenue, Suite 3304
New York, NY 10118-0069 USA
Web site: www.weigl.com

Library of Congress Cataloging-in-Publication Data

Marshall, Diana.
  Aboriginal Australians / Diana Marshall.
      v. cm. -- (Indigenous peoples)
Includes index.
Contents: Where in the world? -- Stories and legends -- Out of the past
-- Social structures -- Law and order -- Celebrating culture --
Communication -- Art and design -- Dressing up -- Food and fun -- Great
ideas -- At issue -- Into the future -- Fascinating facts.
  ISBN 1-59036-121-0 (lib. bdg. : alk. paper)
  1. Australian aborigines--Juvenile literature. [1. Australian
aborigines.] I. Title. II. Series.
  GN665.M273 2004
  305.89'915--dc21
                        2003003960

Printed in the United States of America
1 2 3 4 5 6 7 8 9 0   07 06 05 04 03

Project Coordinator Heather C. Hudak **Design** Terry Paulhus **Layout** Katherine Phillips
Copy Editor Donald Wells **Photo Research** Pamela Wilton and Wendy Cosh

Consultant Dr. Virginia McGowan, PhD (anthropologist)

CONTENTS

Where in the World?

Arnhem Land

Indian Ocean

Kimberley Plateau

Great Sandy Desert

Tanami Desert

Hamersley Range

Macdonnell Rang

Gibson Desert

Simpson Desert

Great Artesian Basin

Musgrave Range

Great Dividing Range

Pacific Ocean

N

Great Victoria Desert

Nullarbor Plain

Darling River

Murray River

Adelaide

Great Dividing Range

Southern Ocean

0   500 Miles

South East Cape

The Commonwealth of Australia is divided into six states and two territories. The states are Western Australia, South Australia, Queensland, New South Wales, Tasmania, and Victoria. The territories are the Northern Territory and the Australian Capital Territory.

The word "aboriginal" means the first people to **inhabit** a land. It is also the name of the **indigenous peoples** of Australia. These Aboriginal Australians are believed to have occupied every region of this **continent**, at one time or another, for more than 50,000 years. Today, Aboriginal Australians live in all states and territories of Australia, with the highest number living in the states of Queensland and New South Wales.

Many different theories explain how Aboriginal Australians first arrived in Australia. Some people believe that a group of people traveled from India to Australia using rafts and canoes thousands of years ago. Sea levels lowered

during the last Ice Age, making the distance between Asia and Australia much shorter and easier to cross. Other people believe the water levels were so low that a bridge of land connected Southeast Asia to Australia. Aboriginal Australians believe that their people have always lived in Australia. The first inhabitants of Australia made a home on its sandy coasts and its harsh

Before the arrival of Europeans, Aboriginal Australians did not have a formal system of land ownership. They did not mark their territories because all members of the group knew the boundaries.

deserts by adapting to the land.

Until 200 years ago, Aboriginal Australians were **nomadic**. Aboriginal Australians understood their environment, and they could survive in the harshest places in Australia. Since the arrival of European settlers in the late

1700s, Aboriginal Australians have been pushed out of the milder **climates** along the coast. Now, they live in the harsh regions known as "the **outback**." In these regions, Aboriginal Australians have learned how to find water in the desert and hunt animals in the bush land and forests.

- Australia is the smallest continent, but the sixth-largest country in the world.

- It is estimated that by the year 2006, there will be 469,000 Aboriginal Australians, about 2.4 percent of the total population of Australia.

- Australia is almost as large as the United States, but it only has a population of about 19.2 million. The United States has more than 290 million people living in it.

- The capital of Australia is Canberra. The largest city is Sydney.

Stories and Legends

Various birds and other animals appear in the Dreamtime stories told by Aboriginal Australians.

Aboriginal culture is based on the concept of the "Dreamtime." The Dreamtime is the time when all things on Earth were created. During the Dreamtime, the Ancestor Spirits journeyed across the **wasteland** that was Earth. As they traveled across the land, they created animals, land, plants, the Moon, the sky, stars, the Sun, and water. When the spirits were finished, they changed into animals, plants, and other objects found on Earth. The places where the spirits settled are known as Dreaming Places. They form the environment in which Aboriginal Australians live. The Dreamtime creation stories explain the origin of the natural world and why these indigenous peoples should live in harmony with it.

Different Aboriginal groups have their own versions of the Dreamtime stories. Each person's or group's stories and beliefs are called "Dreaming." Although the stories are different, they share many of the same Ancestor Spirits. Creation stories often tell of a powerful father figure, known as Biami. He was the main creator who watched over his people, punishing those who broke his laws. During **initiation ceremonies**, Biami spoke to Aboriginal boys who were about to become men. Most Aboriginal groups tell the story of the Rainbow Serpent (also called Great Rainbow Snake or Mother Snake), a creator associated with water and new life. It is believed that as the Rainbow Serpent awoke from her long sleep at the center of Earth, her massive body created tracks in the dirt, which were filled with the rain of her magic. These tracks became lakes, rivers, and **billabongs**. With this water came growth and life.

Indigenous Australians believe there are many **Ancestor** Spirits, such as animal spirits, evil spirits, good spirits, land spirits, plant spirits, and sky spirits. Through the Dreamtime

The koala bear is the main figure in the Dreamtime story called "Illawarra and the Five Islands."

stories, Aboriginal Australians are able to understand how they are related to all other species and objects on Earth.

THE STORY OF THE EMU, THE POSSUM, AND THE KANGAROO

At one time the emu, Waitch, and his uncle, the kangaroo, Quorra, lived together. They often argued about who was the better hunter. The elders decided they should hold a hunting contest to settle the matter. A possum named Koormal would be the prey.

At dawn on the chosen day, Waitch and Quorra set out on the great possum hunt. Quorra was the first to spot Koormal who was in an old gum tree. He quickly trapped the possum and returned home. When Waitch learned he had lost the contest, he became very angry.

After the contest, the elders met and decided to **banish** Waitch for his poor sportsmanship. Quorra felt sorry for his nephew and asked that he be banished as well. Today, all three animals live alone in nature.

Cave paintings by Aboriginal Australians are found across Northern Australia. These paintings usually show hunting scenes and animals.

Out of the Past

Captain James Cook claimed the continent of Australia on behalf of Great Britain in 1770. He named the continent New South Wales.

Early Aboriginal Australians survived by fishing, gathering plant foods, and hunting birds, reptiles, and mammals. Early Aboriginal Australians were **resourceful** people who adapted their lifestyle to fit each new region and climate. As a result, Aboriginal groups were able to spread across the continent. Each group had its own territory and developed its own languages, rituals, and social organizations.

When European settlers began landing on the sandy beaches of Australia in 1788, the indigenous peoples' way of life was disrupted. At the time, there were as many as 1 million Aboriginal Australians calling the island of Australia home.

They belonged to 500 distinct groups and spoke nearly 250 different languages. Today, about 400,000 Aboriginal Australians live in Australia. They speak 100 different languages.

European exploration of the island caused the loss of many Aboriginal Australians' lives and traditions. The first European settlement was in

Traditionally, Aboriginal men hunted large animals such as kangaroos, emus, and turtles.

TIME LINE

10,000–40,000 BC Aboriginal Australians arrive in Australia.

16th and 17th Centuries Dutch, Spanish, French, and British ships sail into Australian waters and **survey** the area.

1770 Captain James Cook claims Australia for England when he lands in eastern Australia.

1788 The first European colony to be established on the island is made up of prisoners from England.

1804–1830 Tasmanian Aboriginal Australians battle British settlers during the Black War.

1850s A gold rush brings many prospectors to Australia. During the rush, many Aboriginal homes and **sacred** sites are destroyed.

1876 The Tasmanian Aboriginal Australians officially disappear with the death of the last islander.

1967 Aboriginal Australians are able to become Australian citizens.

1973 The government sets up the Office of Aboriginal and Torres Strait Islander Affairs.

1976 A law is passed which declares that Aboriginal Australians are entitled to their lands.

1992 Australia's highest court rules that Aboriginal Australians are the original owners of the land.

the area now known as Sydney. At first, contact with Europeans was peaceful. However, the Europeans did not know much about the Aboriginal Australians' way of life, and soon, the two cultures began to fight. European settlers spread new diseases, killing many Aboriginal Australians. New animals were introduced to the land. These animals, such as sheep and cows, dirtied waterholes and destroyed many of the food sources Aboriginal Australians needed to survive. Many Aboriginal Australians were driven away from their homes and treated like wild animals. Aboriginal Australians were denied the right to practice their own culture and traditions. British settlers built villages in the best areas that had clean water, fertile land, and fish. Since Aboriginal Australians had not built permanent houses or farmed the land, Great Britain claimed Australia as a **colony**.

Many Aboriginal Australians tried to defend themselves using force. Traditional weapons used by Aboriginal Australians were no match for the British and their guns. Many Aboriginal Australians lost their lives while trying to protect their homes. One group of British settlers set up camp on the island of Tasmania in 1803. By 1820, many of the island's Aboriginal peoples had been killed or removed.

Social Structures

During ceremonies, Aboriginal Australians perform special dances. Dancers use **click-sticks** to create a beat.

For most indigenous Australians, religious beliefs are based on a sense of belonging. This comes from the view that all living things are related, which links the idea that every living being was created during the Dreamtime. **Spirituality** is based on being responsible for, and respectful to, the land, the sea, the people, and the Aboriginal culture. For Aboriginal Australians, the land is more than just rocks and grass. It is a whole system that supports life. The land is the center of all spirituality. With spirituality at the center of their social structure, they must respect the land.

Each Aboriginal group tells its own Dreaming stories and is linked to a specific Ancestor Spirit. The paths the spirits traveled during the Dreamtime are of great importance to Aboriginal Australians. These paths marked the territory of a group. Each Aboriginal group has a **totem** figure based on its Ancestor Spirit. A totem can be a plant, animal, or natural object connected to the Dreamtime. For example, people of the kangaroo totem are not allowed to kill or eat kangaroos. They perform special ceremonies in the name of the kangaroo.

An Aboriginal child is expected to learn these Dreamtime stories and rules at a very early age, so that they can be passed on to future **generations**. Children are taught storytelling techniques

On ceremonial occasions, Aboriginal Australians decorate their faces and bodies with paints of different colors. These paints can be made using white clay and berries.

and are expected to memorize the stories and songs.

Young Aboriginal Australians learn sacred stories during initiation ceremonies and gatherings. Initiation ceremonies mark the passage of a child into adulthood. For girls, these ceremonies are usually quite simple. For boys, these ceremonies may take several years to complete. They learn the traditions and sacred stories of the group. After a boy completes his final ceremony, he can marry.

While all members of an Aboriginal group are considered equals, the elder members receive the most respect. This is because the elders have the most knowledge to share. Traditional healers often hold a higher status because they are in direct contact with the spirit world. The healer is the link between the Aboriginal world and the spirit world.

THE SEASONS

Aboriginal Australians believe there are as few as two and as many as six seasons, depending on where they live in Australia.

Communication

Identity is very important to an Aboriginal group's survival. Identity comes from the passing of beliefs and traditions from one generation to the next. This is often done through storytelling. Stories are used to educate children about the importance of the land on which they live, how to behave and why, and how to find food and shelter. Starting at a young age, children attend campfire gatherings and take journeys to waterholes, or important landmarks, to listen to stories of their history and culture. When they become adults, it will be their responsibility to pass these stories on to their children. In this way, the identity of a group has been preserved, or kept safe, for thousands of years.

In the past, language was not used to identify different Aboriginal groups. Still, there were differences in the languages they spoke. Most languages spoken by Aboriginal Australians shared basic features. Often, Aboriginal groups that lived close to one another would learn to speak the other group's language. As a result, many Aboriginal Australians were able to speak more than one language.

The message stick was an important way for groups that did not speak the same language to communicate. Before entering a new territory, Aboriginal Australians would hold up a message stick carved with their

Aboriginal Australians are well known for their longstanding rock art tradition. The earliest rock engravings date back more than 30,000 years.

group's totem. These symbols would identify different groups. Using message sticks helped groups communicate and maintain peace.

Sign language was necessary for times when it was important to be silent. For example, it was tradition to be silent during a hunt or during **mourning** and initiation rituals. Instead of speaking, body language and signals were used. Smoke signals were used to communicate over long distances. If two Aboriginal groups were hunting together, one group might send a signal to the other. This signal would represent a message that the groups had agreed on before the hunt.

TOAS

Toas were a special form of communication, only found in the Lake Eyre region of South Australia. Toas were placed in the ground as signposts to other Aboriginal Australians. When an Aboriginal group moved to another camp, they often left toas behind. These toas would contain directions to the next camp. Toas could also be used to tell stories.

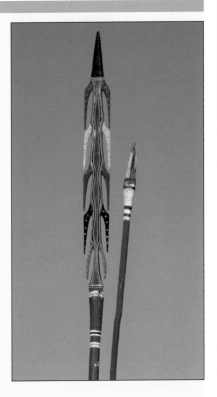

Toas were made out of wood and came in many shapes and sizes. Aboriginal Australians used dyes to decorate the toas. Some toas could be shaped like a river, while others might take the form of an animal. Toas shaped like rivers might be used as a map, with a dot marking the spot where an Aboriginal group was camped.

Traditionally, Aboriginal Australians built small, controlled fires to drive animals into the clearing.

Law and Order

Traditionally, the Aboriginal Australians' relationship with the land governed all actions and behaviors. There were few wars of **conquest**. Each group recognized that different territories were connected to specific Ancestor Spirits. An Aboriginal group would never occupy land that was associated with another group for fear that the spirits would punish them. Even today, many Aboriginal individuals believe that they must be invited to stay in a particular area. It is believed that if they are not welcome, the spirits will punish them.

In Aboriginal culture, all laws were related to the Dreamtime. For Aboriginal Australians, punishment from spirits was considered

The land is a very important part of Aboriginal spirituality. Aboriginal Australians believe they are connected to the land around them.

far worse than the physical punishment associated with human-made laws. The Aboriginal culture does not separate the body from the mind and spirit. All are related through creation. As a result, spiritual punishment affected not only the mind and spirit, but also the body. Laws were created by the spirit world and applied by a healer. There were no police forces or governments. To avoid punishment, all Aboriginal peoples respected each other and nature.

Each Aboriginal group lived according to the Dreaming. The laws of the Dreaming explained many things, such as how much food could be eaten, who each group member should marry, and how members should be educated.

Special roles were given to each member of the group depending on their age and **gender**. Traditionally, women gathered food, and men hunted.

All members of a group were considered **kin**. Kinship relations have certain rights and follow specific behaviors. Group members treated each other as though they were family even if they were not actually related through blood or marriage.

Today, Aboriginal Australians' traditional ways of life and law are being combined with newer forms of government and politics. Aboriginal Australians received the right to vote in 1967. This decision gave Aboriginal Australians the ability to represent themselves in political systems. The Office of Aboriginal and Torres Strait Islander Affairs was created to ensure Aboriginal Australians' lands, political, and social needs are being addressed in culturally appropriate ways.

In some cases, traditional punishment for wrongdoings included tribal spearings or other forms of wounding.

Celebrating Culture

For thousands of years, Aboriginal Australians have preserved their ancient traditions by living in the same ways as their ancestors. Through sacred ceremonies, Aboriginal Australians celebrate their origins and honor the Dreamtime.

Aboriginal Australians are not allowed to talk or write about many of their ceremonies because they are sacred rituals. However, all ceremonies are related to keeping the stories of the Dreamtime alive. In each community, there are people whose job it is to remember the Dreamtime stories. They must memorize every part of the story and its ceremony to pass on to future generations.

During ceremonies, Aboriginal Australians perform the Dreamtime stories. Often, men act as the keeper of a Dreamtime site. Their job is to ensure the area is properly cared for and the Ancestor Spirit is able to continue living at the site. Women act as the keepers of knowledge. They have spiritual and religious power.

Aboriginal Australians hold many different types of ceremonies. Some ceremonies are performed for men only. Others are acted out for women only. Sometimes, Aboriginal Australians hold private ceremonies to which only a few members of a community were invited. Other times, ceremonies

Stories, traditions, and knowledge are passed down from one generation to the next in Aboriginal culture. For example, young boys are taught to hunt at an early age.

are big events involving an entire community.

Music plays an important role in ceremonies. Aboriginal Australians perform sacred songs and dances during ceremonies. They also create sacred symbols such as carvings in wood or clay, **body adornment**, or rock art.

Today, bands such Yothu Yindi promote Aboriginal culture by sharing traditional ceremonial music and dances with the world. Yothu Yindi has both Aboriginal and non-Aboriginal members. The musical group combines the sounds of rock and roll music with traditional Aboriginal Australian music that is thousands of years old.

The Aboriginal members of Yothu Yindi come from settlement areas on the northeast coast of Australia's Northern Territory. Yothu Yindi brings Aboriginal Australians' traditions to other cultures by performing songs, dances, and ceremonies. Each song and dance celebrates Aboriginal Australians' spiritual connection with the land.

17

Art and Culture

Aboriginal Australians used art to express their beliefs and spiritual ideas. Places of worship were chosen because they had a connection to the Dreamtime stories. Places of worship might include a watering hole, an **outcropping** of rock, or a grove of trees. Much Aboriginal Australian art was inspired by these important places. During traditional **corroborees**, men would paint their bodies with ochers and wear emu feathers. Stories were told through song and dance. These were performed to the rhythm of hand clapping and click-sticks. Whenever an important event happened, Aboriginal groups decided how to record the story. Then, it would be memorized and performed.

Aboriginal Australian art was often inspired by nature. Aboriginal Australians painted or engraved images on rock and bark or carved designs into wood. Rock art is the most common art form practiced by Aboriginal Australians. The images of animals, plants, spirits, and totems were painted on caves, cliffs, and rocks. Animals were an important part of Aboriginal culture, and they would often include animal images in their art. The "**x-ray**" painting technique was an ancient art form in which Aboriginal Australians would draw the skeleton of an animal on a rock.

Earthworks, wood carvings, and bark paintings told the stories of the spiritual and natural worlds. These drawings included images of animals, landmarks, and

This painting, called "Gangi Nganang," or "First Miiriwung Men," is drawn on an overhanging rock in Keep River National Park.

Participation in ceremonies and rituals helps young Aboriginal Australians understand their culture's laws and stories.

growth attracted animals for hunting. At least half of the food eaten by Aboriginal Australians came from plants. In the summer months, they ate many fruits and vegetables. In the winter, they ate plant roots. Aboriginal Australians also ate insects, such as ants, bees, grubs, and moths. Insects were used in medicines and foods, too.

For Aboriginal Australians, sports and entertainment were connected to survival and tradition. Children and adults took part in activities such as climbing, jumping, running, and throwing. Games such as skipping and swinging were played for fun. Aboriginal groups competed against one another in contests such as animal tracking, **boomerang** throwing, swimming, tree climbing, and wrestling.

For fun, children often imitated adult activities. Children played with dolls made of twigs and clay. They would pretend to be either the mother or the father. Girls played with smaller versions of their mother's digging sticks.

Boys practiced throwing small spears. Aboriginal children often played ball games, climbed trees, and held races. Most activities made use of the natural landscape, such as skipping stones across water surfaces.

Aboriginal Australians made body decorations such as headbands, bracelets, necklaces, and pendants. They also made crafts from animal teeth and bones, feathers, shells, and woven fibers.

Great Ideas

Aboriginal culture is deeply connected to the natural world. Using natural resources, Aboriginal Australians have made many items. These items helped them adapt to their environment. For example, Aboriginal Australians did not live in houses. Instead, during the mosquito season, they built huts of grass and bark. They lit small fires inside the huts to drive the insects away. In windy regions, they built walls of tree and stone, called windbreaks. These windbreaks would shield the village from gusts of wind.

The didgeridoo is a traditional instrument that Aboriginal Australians play during celebrations, corroborees, and rituals. The didgeridoo was a long, cone-shaped, wooden horn.

A didgeridoo was made from a branch of a tree that had been hollowed out by termites. The bark was removed from the hollowed branch. Hot coals or a stick were used to clean out the

Didgeridoos are made from trees hollowed out by termites. The harvesting of trees to make this instrument must be carefully timed. This ensures the didgeridoo is the proper thickness.

branch. The smaller end of the branch was coated with beeswax to make a mouthpiece. The didgeridoo was painted with the group's designs and totems. A person would blow into the mouthpiece to make a sound. The sound a didgeridoo made depended on the length and width of the branch.

Aboriginal Australians still use the didgeridoo to play songs for different ceremonies. For example, they play Dreaming songs, funeral songs, and hunting songs.

The boomerang is one item that displayed Aboriginal Australians' woodworking skills. The boomerang was a curved, flat, wooden weapon used to hunt and defend. When thrown, the boomerang would soar more than 295 feet (90 meters) in the air. It would then circle around and return to the thrower. This item allowed Aboriginal men to hunt animals from a safe distance. When thrown into a flock of birds, a boomerang looked like a hawk. Often, as the birds tried to escape the hawk, they would fly into the hunter's nets. Aboriginal Australians made many other items from natural resources, such as clubs, digging sticks, shields, spears, and throwing sticks.

Many other cultures hunted with non-returning throwing sticks, but the boomerang is unique to Aboriginal Australia.

THE RETURNING STICK

A boomerang returns to its thrower because of its special design. A boomerang has two wings, which allow it to spin around the center bend. The two wings are designed like the wings of an airplane—the bottoms are flat and the tops are rounded. Air flows differently around the bottom than the top, creating a lift. When the wings spin, one wing pushes the boomerang forward and one wing pulls it backward. At a certain point, the boomerang stops moving forward and starts moving backward. Not everyone can make a boomerang return. It takes practice to throw it just right.

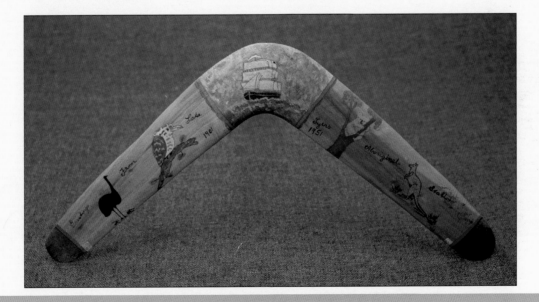

At Issue

When European settlers first arrived in Australia, they failed to understand the relationship Aboriginal Australians share with the land. For hundreds of years, this relationship has been misunderstood. This relationship is at the center of all the issues facing Aboriginal Australians today.

When the government forced Aboriginal Australians from their land, their culture and survival were placed in danger. They lost many of the medicines and foods they relied on for survival because they were no longer able to maintain their relationship with the natural world. Today, Aboriginal Australians are

speaking to the government about regaining their land and rights. In 1990, the Australian government created the Aboriginal and Torres Strait Islander Commission (ATSIC). Members are elected to ATSIC to represent the indigenous peoples of Australia. ATSIC made laws to help Aboriginal Australians claim land and

Uluru is the Aboriginal Australian name for Ayers Rock. Uluru is located in Uluru-Kata Tjuta National Park in the Northern Territory. In 1985, the park land was returned to the Aboriginal Australians, who then leased the land to the Australian National Parks and Wildlife Service.

social protection. Laws now exist allowing Aboriginal groups to govern their own territory. ATSIC also receives funding from the government to aid with community human development, housing, and maintaining cultural identity. Sacred sites are being protected from the dangers of development, industry, and mining. In 1985, a group of Aboriginal artists created a poster which demanded that Ayers Rock and the surrounding area be returned to its original owners. The land rights to this tourist attraction were returned, and its name was changed to *Uluru*. Aboriginal Australians believe the rock is the spiritual heart of Australia.

Today, Aboriginal Australians are asking that their culture and heritage be preserved. They are taking action and working to save their traditional beliefs and ways of life. In 1938, a group of Aboriginal Australians gathered to declare a Day of Mourning for the treatment of their people. Since then, Aboriginal Australians have been advocating for **civil rights**. Struggling against years of **racism**, many Aboriginal groups are trying to change the way other Australian citizens views them.

In Australia, the government is making changes to ensure Aboriginal Australians no longer endure racist attitudes as they did in the past. Aboriginal organizations are working with the Australian government to strengthen and improve living conditions. ATSIC and many other land councils are working together to build a peaceful relationship between Aboriginal Australians and other Australian citizens.

AUSTRALIA DAY PROTEST

On January 26, 1988, many Australians were celebrating Australia Day. This day marked the 200th anniversary of the arrival of the first European settlers. For most Australians, it was a time to honor the achievements of these settlers. For Aboriginal Australians, it was a time of mourning. Aboriginal Australians call this day Invasion Day—the day when Europeans began stealing their culture, land, and lifestyle. To protest Australia Day, tens of thousands of Aboriginal Australians marched to Sydney Harbour in one of the largest gatherings in their history. Their actions forced other Australians to learn more about their concerns.

Into the Future

With support from the Australian government, Aboriginal Australians have built many art centers. The Injalak Arts Center in the Northern Territory is one of many centers that offers both art supplies and housing to indigenous peoples who want to practice traditional and modern art forms. The art created at these centers is sold to local galleries. Aboriginal artists also get a portion of the sale price. While artists benefit from the money they receive, the larger community benefits by learning about Aboriginal culture and traditions.

Aboriginal beliefs, strengths, and traditions are a source of inspiration for Aboriginal artists.

Thancoupie is a well-known Aboriginal artist. She is a ceramic artist who is known around the world for her work. Thancoupie is known for making clay forms, which feature designs from her own culture and from the Dreamtime. Her art serves to help future generations remember the traditional stories and myths of

Aboriginal Australians preserve their cultural traditions through art.

Aboriginal Australians. Thancoupie represented Australia in the 2000 San Paolo Art Biennial in Brazil.

Sally Morgan is a painter and writer who researched her family history to learn more about her Aboriginal ancestry. Her books and paintings have won many awards.

Jack Davis was an Aboriginal **activist**, actor, playwright, and poet. He used his own battle with racism as inspiration for his art. He joined the Aboriginal Advancement Council to help fight for changes in government policies. He gained international recognition for his art and work as an activist. Davis died in 2000.

Since the 1970s, many Aboriginal Australians have moved away from towns and cities to live in small, isolated communities called outstations.

Mudrooroo Nyoongah is the author of many stories, including "Doctor Wooreddy's Prescription for Enduring the Ending of the World." In 1965, he published his first novel, which was titled *Wildcat Falling*. This was the first book ever published by an Aboriginal writer. In 1975, the book was made into a film.

CATHY FREEMAN

Cathy Freeman is a national hero among all Australians. At the age of 16, she became the first Aboriginal Australian sprinter to win a gold medal at the Commonwealth Games. At the 1992 Summer Olympics in Atlanta, Georgia, Freeman became the first Aboriginal Australian track and field athlete to represent Australia in the Olympic Games.

In the 2000 Summer Olympics in Sydney, Australia, Freeman was given the honor of lighting the Olympic Cauldron during the opening ceremonies. During the Sydney Olympics, Freeman won the gold medal in the 400-meter race. The gold medal win was a great moment for her country—it was Australia's 100th Olympic gold medal.

Fascinating Facts

- Australia is home to the ten most poisonous snakes in the world. The inland taipan has enough venom in just one bite to kill 100 people.

- Most of Australia's mammals are **marsupials**, including the kangaroo, koala bear, wallaby, and wombat.

- The most poisonous spider in the world is found in Australia. The Sydney funnel web spider's fangs can pierce through a human fingernail.

- Australia is both the world's largest island and the world's smallest continent.

- Aboriginal Australians covered their bodies with animal fat to protect against insect bites.

- Uluru is the largest single rock in the world. Most of the rock is hidden beneath the ground.

- The Aboriginal flag was made the official flag of Aboriginal peoples on July 14, 1995. Harold Thomas designed the flag, and it has been in use since July 12, 1971.

- The expression "three dog night" is an Australian term. As the story goes, during cold nights, people would need three dingoes to keep from freezing.

- Many Aboriginal groups ate moths and bees, which taste like sweet nuts when roasted.

- Europeans banned Aboriginal stories from being told until early in the twentieth century.

FURTHER READING

Anne Bartlett. *The Aboriginal People of Australia (First Peoples)*. Minneapolis: Lerner Publications Company, 2001.

Maralngura, N., and Bill M. J. Bunter. *Djugurba: Tales from the Spirit Time*. Bloomington: Indiana University Press, 1976.

WEB SITES

Aboriginal Art Online www.aboriginalartonline.com

Aboriginal and Torres Strait Islander Commission www.atsic.gov.au

Glossary

activist a person who believes strongly in political or social change and tries to make changes happen

ancestor a person, plant, animal, or object from a past generation

banish to force out of a place

billabongs low areas of ground that were once rivers

body adornment the practice of decorating the body with symbols and designs to express beliefs and identity

boomerang curved throwing stick invented by Aboriginal Australians

bullroarers instruments made from a thin, flat piece of wood attached to a string; makes a howling or roaring sound when it is spun

civil rights the rights given to a person in a society

click-sticks two small sticks that are hit together to create a beat

climates general weather conditions for specific places

cloaks loose pieces of clothing that fasten around the neck

colony a country or area that is controlled by a more powerful country

conquest to gain control of something

continent one of Earth's seven large areas of land, including Africa, Antarctica, Asia, Australia, Europe, North America, and South America

corroborees celebrations that are usually held at night, at which time Aboriginal Australians tell stories using songs and dances

cycad palm tree

earthworks large designs made from raised earth or mud

gender being male or female

generations people of the same age living in a society or family

identity the qualities by which a person or group is known

indigenous peoples the first, or original, inhabitants of a particular region or country

inhabit to live in a place

initiation ceremonies processes by which someone becomes part of a group

kin family members or relatives

marsupials mammals that are carried in a pouch on their mother's body until they are fully developed

mourning feeling sadness over someone's death

nomadic a tendency to move from place to place

outback the large middle region of Australia that is a dry and semi-desert area

outcropping a large rock or group of rocks that sticks out from surrounding rocks

racism the belief that one race is better than another race

resourceful able to solve problems quickly and easily

sacred things that are spiritual, religious, and holy

spirituality having deep feelings and beliefs about something that is not part of the physical world

survey to find out the area and shape of a piece of land and record the details

totem an object or being that is the symbol of a group or family; religious symbol

wasteland an area of land where there are no living things or buildings

x-ray a picture of a skeleton

31

Index

Photograph Credits

Every reasonable effort has been made to trace ownership and to obtain permission to reprint copyright material. The publishers would be pleased to have any errors or omissions brought to their attention so that they may be corrected in subsequent printings.

Cover: Aboriginal boy (Oz Outback/Ludo Kuipers); **Auscape International:** pages 13T (Jean-Paul Ferrero), 22T (Reg Morrison), 22B (Sorrel Wilby & Chris Ciantar), 23 (Wayne Lawler), 30 (Reg Morrison); **Bill Bachman:** pages 1, 24; **Corel Corporation:** pages 5, 6, 7L, 7R, 7B, 11B, 16, 19B, 26, 28, 29T; **Matthew McKee; Eye Ubiquitous/CORBIS:** page 27; **National Archives of Australia:** page 29B; **National Library of Australia:** pages 8 (Samuel Calvert - an7682920), 9 (Joseph Lycett, - an2962844), 13B (Joseph Lycett - an2962939), 15 (Joseph Lycett - an2962947), 21B (John William Lindt - ac10642263-3), 25 (an7726265-v); **Steven Nowakowski:** page 21T; **OZ Outback/Ludo Kuipers:** pages 10, 18; **Photos.com:** page 3; **Skyscans/David C. Hancock:** pages 11T, 12, 14, 17, 19T, 20.